The Story Begins

Experiencing God's Story Series

The Story Begins: The Authority of the Bible, the Triune God, the Great and Good God

The Hero Who Restores: Humanity, Satan and Sin, Jesus Christ

The Rescue: Salvation, the Holy Spirit, the Church

New People Forever: Transformation, Mission, the End

Experiencing God's Story #1

The Story Begins

The Authority of the Bible, the Triune God, the Great and Good God

J. Scott Duvall

Kregel
Publications

The Story Begins: The Authority of the Bible, the Triune God, the Great and Good God

© 2009 by J. Scott Duvall

Published by Kregel Publications, a division of Kregel, Inc., P.O. Box 2607, Grand Rapids, MI 49501.

This material is also published as part of a workbook under the title *Experiencing God's Story of Life and Hope: A Workbook for Spiritual Formation,* © 2008 and published by Kregel Publications.

All Scripture quotations, unless otherwise indicated, are from the *Holy Bible, New International Version®.* Copyright © 1973, 1978, 1984 by International Bible Society. Used by permission of Zondervan. All rights reserved.

Scripture quotations marked NASB are from the NEW AMERICAN STANDARD BIBLE, updated edition. Copyright © 1960, 1962, 1963, 1968, 1971, 1972, 1973, 1975, 1977, 1995 by The Lockman Foundation. Used by permission. (www.Lockman.org)

Italics used in various Scripture quotations has been added by the author for emphasis.

ISBN 978-0-8254-2595-0

Printed in the United States of America

09 10 11 12 13 / 5 4 3 2 1

CONTENTS

I would like to thank the following people for their help in developing this resource: Brandon O'Brien, Josh and Jill McCarty, Michael and Terese Cox, Julie (Byrum) Stone, Kristine (Lewis) Smith, and Brandon Holiski. The other pastoral leaders at Fellowship Church—Scott Jackson, Neal Nelson, and Darrell Bridges—have been very encouraging throughout the process. My daughter Meagan spent hours sitting in my office punching holes in each page and compiling the first round of books. Thanks, everyone!

Read Me First

Whether you were raised in the church and accepted Christ as your personal savior at age five, or whether you have only recently given your life to Christ, spiritual growth is not optional. God expects his children to *grow up!*

We define *spiritual formation* as the process of allowing God to conform us to the image of Jesus Christ. The Bible clearly teaches that God wants his children to grow to maturity. As you read the sampling of verses below, especially notice the italicized words.

> For those God foreknew he also predestined to be *conformed to the likeness of his Son*, that he might be the firstborn among many brothers. (Rom. 8:29)

> Therefore, I urge you, brothers, in view of God's mercy, to offer your bodies as living sacrifices, holy and pleasing to God—this is your spiritual act of worship. Do not conform any longer to the pattern of this world, but *be transformed* by the renewing of your mind. Then you will be able to test and approve what God's will is—his good, pleasing and perfect will. (Rom. 12:1–2)

> And we, who with unveiled faces all reflect the Lord's glory, are *being transformed into his likeness* with ever-increasing glory, which comes from the Lord, who is the Spirit. (2 Cor. 3:18)

> Therefore we do not lose heart. Though outwardly we are wasting away, yet inwardly *we are being renewed* day by day. (2 Cor. 4:16)

> My dear children, for whom I am again in the pains of childbirth *until Christ is formed in you* . . . (Gal. 4:19)

> You were taught, with regard to your former way of life, to put off your old self, which is being corrupted by its deceitful desires; to *be made new* in the attitude of your minds; and to put on the new self, *created to be like God* in true righteousness and holiness. (Eph. 4:22–24)

. . . being confident of this, that *he who began a good work in you will carry it on to completion* until the day of Christ Jesus. (Phil. 1:6)

Therefore, my dear friends, as you have always obeyed—not only in my presence, but now much more in my absence—continue to *work out your salvation* with fear and trembling, *for it is God who works in you* to will and to act according to his good purpose. (Phil. 2:12–13)

Have nothing to do with godless myths and old wives' tales; rather, *train yourself to be godly.* (1 Tim. 4:7)

Like newborn babies, crave pure spiritual milk, so that by it *you may grow up in your salvation*, now that you have tasted that the Lord is good. (1 Peter 2:2–3)

Each aspect of our definition of *spiritual formation* is significant. Spiritual formation is a *process*. We don't experience growth as a neat, clean, upward slope toward heaven. In reality it looks and feels more like a roller-coaster ride, twisting and turning and looping and climbing and dropping. Only as you stand back and see the big picture can you tell that the "exit" to the ride is higher than the "entrance." Spiritual formation is a messy process. Because we don't always cooperate with the Lord, it takes time for him to accomplish his purpose in our lives. Philippians 1:6 offers a great deal of encouragement here (see above). God never stops working.

Spiritual formation is the process of *allowing* God to work in our lives. God is sovereign but he has also created us to make important decisions and to bear the responsibility for those decisions. We have no power in and of ourselves to cause our own growth, nor will God force us to obey him. We must allow God to work in our lives and to bring about change. God deeply desires to work, but we must give him the necessary time and space. We don't cause our own growth, but we do cooperate with God as he works. Check out Philippians 2:12–13 above.

Spiritual formation is a process of allowing *God* to work in our lives. We are told that the Holy Spirit continues the earthly ministry that Jesus began (Acts 1:1–2). God's Spirit lives within each genuine believer (1 Cor. 6:19). Our growth is not the result of special circumstances or good luck. We don't grow by our own willpower or by striving to obey the Law. We grow when we follow the Holy Spirit, who alone can produce spiritual fruit in our lives (see Gal. 5:16–23). For us to be loving, joyful, peaceful, and so on, the Holy Spirit must be allowed to do his work.

Spiritual formation is the process of allowing God *to conform us* to the image of Jesus. As much as I hate to admit it, growth means change. Like clay in the potter's hand, we are shaped and molded and conformed to a particular pattern. Change at the hand of God is sometimes painful, but it is always good. We don't always like it, but deep down we always desire it because we know it is necessary. James tells us to "consider it pure joy . . . whenever you face trials of many kinds, because you know that the testing of your faith develops perseverance" and "perseverance must finish its work so that you may be mature and complete, not lacking anything" (James 1:2–4). God loves us too much to let us stay as we are.

Finally, spiritual formation is the process of allowing God to conform us *to the image of Jesus Christ.* In Romans 8:29; 2 Corinthians 3:18; and Galatians 4:19 (see page 9), we are told that God is making us more and more like his Son. Jesus is the perfect pattern or model. He represents the goal of spiritual formation. We are not being shaped into merely religious people or ethical people or church-going people. We are being conformed to the very character of Christ himself.

Everyone, without exception, experiences some kind of "spiritual formation." Dallas Willard puts it this way:

> All people undergo a process of spiritual formation. Their spirit is formed, and with it their whole being. . . . Spiritual formation is not something just for especially religious people. No one escapes. The most hardened criminal as well as the most devout of human beings have had a spiritual formation. They have become a certain kind of person. You have had a spiritual formation and I have had one, and it is still ongoing. It is like education: everyone gets one—a good one or a bad one. (*Renovation of the Heart,* 45)

Everyone is being formed by certain powers after a particular pattern or model. We are blessed beyond words to be able to participate in God's design for spiritual formation.

God often uses resources to shape or mold us into conformity with Christ's character. Of course, the primary resource is God's Word, the Bible. But there are also many good and helpful supplementary resources. We certainly know that no ministry resource of any kind can ever substitute for a personal relationship with God through Jesus Christ, but God does seem to use spiritual-growth resources to help our love for him grow deeper and stronger. The Experiencing God's Story series is one particularly effective resource that God can use to help us understand and participate consistently in true, godly spiritual formation.

Believing-Behaving-Becoming

Most resources focus on just one aspect of the spiritual formation process. Some tools emphasize our *beliefs* by explaining the core teachings of the Christian faith. Knowing what to believe is crucial, but there is more. Many spiritual formation resources highlight how we should *behave.* They stress the importance of spiritual disciplines such as prayer, Bible study, solitude, worship, and so on. Without a doubt God uses such disciplines to transform our lives, but the disciplines are means to an end, not the end themselves.

The disciplines are like workout routines pointing toward the game itself. The game is our life with God. Finally, there are a handful of resources that pay attention to what people are *becoming* in the entire process of spiritual formation (i.e., godly character). Most of these center on the fruit of the Spirit as the true test of spirituality, and rightly so.

The Experiencing God's Story series connects all three aspects of spiritual formation: what we believe, how we behave, and who we are becoming. All three are essential to our growth:

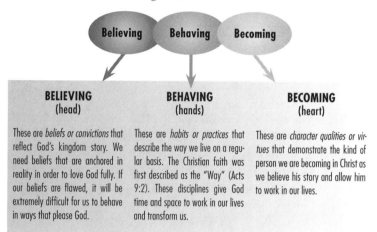

BELIEVING (head)	**BEHAVING** (hands)	**BECOMING** (heart)
These are *beliefs or convictions* that reflect God's kingdom story. We need beliefs that are anchored in reality in order to love God fully. If our beliefs are flawed, it will be extremely difficult for us to behave in ways that please God.	These are *habits or practices* that describe the way we live on a regular basis. The Christian faith was first described as the "Way" (Acts 9:2). These disciplines give God time and space to work in our lives and transform us.	These are *character qualities or virtues* that demonstrate the kind of person we are becoming in Christ as we believe his story and allow him to work in our lives.

As a teaching tool, each workbook in this series connects a "Believing" area with a "Behaving" area and a "Becoming" area. Look at the overview on pages 16–17 to see the whole plan. For example, in the third row of the overview you will notice a belief in a great and good God. That belief is connected to the habit of worship and to the quality of purity or holiness. In other words, each row of the overview is connected and integrated; each belief is tied to a behavior or habit and then to a character quality.

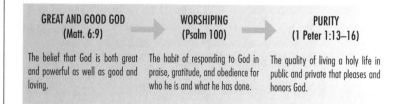

GREAT AND GOOD GOD (Matt. 6:9)	**WORSHIPING** (Psalm 100)	**PURITY** (1 Peter 1:13–16)
The belief that God is both great and powerful as well as good and loving.	The habit of responding to God in praise, gratitude, and obedience for who he is and what he has done.	The quality of living a holy life in public and private that pleases and honors God.

This Believing-Behaving-Becoming arrangement is merely a teaching tool and is not intended as a rigid religious system. Sometimes beliefs lead to behavior, while at other times behavior influences beliefs. I'm not suggesting a 1-2-3, neat, clean, foolproof, linear progression that will solve all of life's problems. We all know that life is messy, dynamic, unpredictable, confusing, spontaneous, mystical, and so on. But I still think there are important connections to be made using this teaching arrangement. For instance, what we believe about Satan and sin will affect how we fight spiritual battles and how we understand and experience true freedom. While recognizing this somewhat artificial organization, I hope the Believing-Behaving-Becoming setup encourages you to allow the Lord to work in your entire life rather than just one area of your life.

The four study guides in this series include a total of thirty-six boxes of beliefs, behaviors, and character qualities.

Why these particular topics? Were they chosen simply because they are the most popular topics when it comes to spiritual growth? Are we looking at a random bunch of beliefs and habits and virtues all loosely connected? Actually, the topics were not chosen at random or through some popularity contest. These topics reflect God's story and in our context today we definitely need to stay anchored to God's story.

Experiencing God's Story of Life and Hope

Since the late 1960s we have been experiencing a cultural shift from modernism to postmodernism. (See Jimmy Long's excellent book *Emerging Hope* for more on this cultural change and how Christians can respond.) The modern era emphasized the individual, objective truth, words, and some kind of grand story to explain the meaning of life. By contrast, the postmodern era emphasizes community, subjective "truth," images, and the absence of any grand story to explain life. Christians can embrace some aspects of postmodernism and probably need to resist others. For instance, we can certainly celebrate the greater emphasis on community. But if we give up on a big story that explains reality, then we might as well give up on our faith.

The Christian faith is founded upon God's grand story revealed in the Bible. Postmodernism does away with all big stories that claim to explain reality, opting instead for local or small-group stories. What is true for me and my friends is what is true—period! But Christians can't abandon God's grand story or there is nothing left to believe and all hope is lost. Instead, we need to understand God's story even more and see how it connects to life and how it does us good. We would say that what is real and true is not just what my local group prefers, but what God has revealed. God's story explains life.

Spiritual formation needs to be connected to God's story or it can be manipulated to mean almost anything. In other words, we need a biblical story approach to spiritual formation. But we obviously need to do more than just "believe" the story. We need to act upon the story and allow God's story to shape our whole being. Perhaps now the title makes more sense. We need to experience (beliefs, habits, character qualities) God's story (as revealed in the Bible) of life and hope (a story that does what is best for us).

How is this story approach built into these workbooks? It's simple. If you look again at the overview you will notice that the "Believing" column is actually God's grand story.

BELIEVING	(meaning in the story)
Authority of the Bible	A trustworthy script for the story
Triune God who is Great and Good	Begins with God who is community
Humanity	God wants to share his community
Satan and Sin	Evil powers try to ruin the plan
Jesus Christ	The hero of the story
Salvation	The rescue begins
Holy Spirit	God with us until the end
The Church	The community being rescued
Transformation	God works among his children
Mission	God works through his children
The End	The end—we are with God in the new creation

The very first item in the column is the *Bible* or the script of the story. The story proper begins with *God*—who he is and what he has done. God creates *human beings* to relate to him in perfect community, but *Satan and sin* spoil God's good creation and interfere with his story. God must now attempt a rescue to save his creation. Because of his great love for us, God sent his Son *Jesus Christ* to rescue us from Satan and sin and restore us to a relationship with him. *Salvation* means that God has come to rescue us from the dark side. Through Christ, God offers us a way home. As we respond to his gracious offer by trusting him, we are adopted by God into his family. He puts his very own *Spirit* within us and incorporates us into his community. God desires to use this *new community* (called *church*) to provide us with identity, stability, and wholeness. As we eat, pray, worship, and listen to God's Word together, we begin to feel safe. We open up, revealing our joys and struggles. We discover that we can really be known and loved at the same time, rather than just one or the other. Perhaps for the first time we experience life and hope through Christ and his community. We are *transformed* into the kind of person we were created to be. Naturally, we want other people to experience this life and hope. We have a *mission*— to live out God's story in biblical community so that others can join God's community. Since it is a story of hope, God's story *ends* happily (read Rev. 21:1–4).

To summarize, the "Believing" column is God's grand story. Spiritual formation is anchored in God's story. As we move through the story (from top to bottom), each Belief area extends out (from left to right) to a Behaving and a Becoming area. In this way our whole life is being shaped by the Lord and the entire process is firmly secured to God's story.

Workbook Format

Most of the studies in these workbooks consist of the following elements:

- An introduction that explores the biblical context
- "A Closer Look," to dig deeper into a particular text
- "Crossing the Bridge," to move from the ancient world to our world
- "So What?" to apply what we have discovered in the context of biblical community
- "The Power of Words," to help you understand the meaning of words in the text
- Insightful quotes that inspire reflection and action
- Application questions for your small group
- Cross-references for more Bible exploration
- A "For Deeper Study" recommended reading list

In terms of assumptions, characteristics, and benefits, the Experiencing God's Story series is:

- theologically grounded in the evangelical Christian tradition
- spiritually integrated by connecting believing, behaving, and becoming
- academically reliable through the use of solid biblical scholarship
- pedagogically interactive without being insulting (i.e., you won't find rhetorical fill-in-the-blank questions)
- creatively designed to be used by individuals within the context of biblical community
- practically and realistically arranged into four books, each with 3 three-part chapters

Another subtle characteristic worth mentioning is that the workbooks teach by example how to do responsible Bible study. The move from context to observation to theological principle to application follows the journey model detailed in *Grasping God's Word* by Scott Duvall and Daniel Hays.

May the Lord bless you richly as you allow him to conform you to the image of Jesus Christ. I pray that the Experiencing God's Story series will serve you well on your journey.

Overview of the Experiencing God's Story Series

	BELIEVING	BEHAVING	BECOMING
The Story Begins	**Authority of the Bible** (2 Tim. 3:16–17) The belief that the Bible is God's inspired Word given to us to help us mature in our faith.	**Studying the Bible** (2 Tim. 2:15) The habit of reading, interpreting, and applying the Bible as the primary means of listening to God.	**Truth** (Eph. 4:20–25) The quality of living and speaking truthfully in a world of lies and deception.
	Triune God (Gal. 4:4–6) The belief that the Bible teaches the triune (three-in-one) nature of God.	**Fellowshiping** (Acts 2:42–47) The habit of living in authentic relationship with and dependence upon other followers of Jesus.	**Love** (1 John 4:7–8) The quality of choosing to do what God says is best for another person.
	Great and Good God (Matt. 6:9) The belief that God is both great and powerful as well as good and loving.	**Worshiping** (Psalm 100) The habit of responding to God in praise, gratitude, and obedience for who he is and what he has done.	**Purity** (1 Peter 1:13–16) The quality of living a holy life in public and private that pleases and honors God.
The Hero Who Restores	**Humanity** (Gen. 1:26–28) The belief that human beings are uniquely created in the image of God.	**Seeking the Kingdom** (Matt. 6:33) The habit of acknowledging that God is our Creator and that we are creatures intended to seek him and his purposes.	**Rest** (Matt. 11:28–30) The quality of living with a deep awareness of and contentment with God's purpose for our lives.
	Satan and Sin (Gen. 3:1–7) The belief that Satan is the leader of the opposition against God and his people, and that all human beings have a willful opposition to God's claim on their lives (sin).	**Waging Spiritual War** (Matt. 4:1–11) The habit of knowing and using appropriate strategies for fighting against the Devil, the flesh, and the world.	**Freedom** (Rom. 8:1–4) The quality of experiencing freedom from Satan's power and sin's domination and freedom for new life with God.
	Jesus Christ (John 1:1–3, 14, 18) The belief that Jesus Christ is God the Son, fully divine and fully human.	**Following** (Mark 8:34–38) The habit of daily choosing to follow Jesus Christ as Lord in every area of life.	**New Identity in Christ** (John 21:15–23) The quality of single-minded allegiance to Jesus Christ above every other competing loyalty.

BELIEVING	BEHAVING	BECOMING	
Salvation (Eph. 2:8–10) The belief that salvation is by grace (source), through faith (means), for good works (result).	**Trusting and Acting** (Phil. 2:12–13) The habit of allowing God to work in our lives so that our faith results in action (not salvation by works, but true faith that works).	**Assurance** (Rom. 8:15–16) The quality of knowing (with a healthy confidence) that we belong to God.	**The Rescue**
Holy Spirit (John 14:16–17) The belief that God the Spirit continues Jesus' earthly ministry, especially that of transforming believers and empowering them to fulfill their mission.	**Walking by the Spirit** (Gal. 5:16, 25) The habit of living in dependence upon the Holy Spirit as the source of strength to resist temptation and imitate Jesus Christ.	**Fruit of the Spirit** (Gal. 5:22–24) The quality of bearing the fruit of the Holy Spirit (Christlike character qualities) in one's life.	
The Church (1 Peter 2:4–10) The belief that God's people are joined together in Christ into a new community, the church.	**Serving** (Mark 10:35–45) The habit of being a servant to other members of this new community.	**Humility** (Luke 18:9–14) The quality of a servant's attitude grounded in the recognition of our status before God and our relationship to others.	
Transformation (Rom. 12:1–2) The belief that we are not to be conformed to this world, but we are to be transformed into the image of Jesus Christ.	**Praying** (Matt. 6:9–13) The habit of continual communion with God that fosters our relationship and allows for genuine transformation in our lives.	**Peace** (Phil. 4:6–7) The quality of calmness and well being (vs. worry and inner turmoil) that comes as a result of our communion with God.	**New People Forever**
Mission (Matt. 28:18–20) The belief that Jesus commissioned his church to make disciples of all nations.	**Engaging the World** (Acts 1:7–8) The habit of engaging the world for the purpose of sharing the good news of Jesus Christ.	**Compassion** (Luke 10:30–37) The quality of extending love and compassion to people in need.	
The End (1 Thess. 4:13–18) The belief that Jesus Christ will return to judge evil, restore his creation, and live forever in intimate fellowship with his people.	**Persevering** (Heb. 12:1–2) The habit of enduring and persisting in spite of the trials and difficulties we face in life.	**Hope** (Rom. 8:22–25) The quality of a confident expectation that in the end God will be true to his word and keep his promises.	

God Talk

Authority of the Bible

I've never been scuba diving, but I'm told that it's a blast. Strapping on those life tanks and exploring the water world below sounds like fun. Of course it's not all fun and games. A former Navy diver once told me that he had been in waters so deep and dark that it was almost impossible to keep from becoming disoriented and confused. What a terrifying feeling it must be—being under water, unable to see your hands in front of your face, not knowing which way is up, panic engulfing you. I immediately interrupted my friend. "So what did you do?" I knew he had survived the ordeal since he was standing there talking to me. "Feel the bubbles," he said. "When it's pitch black and you have no idea which way to go, you reach up with your hand and feel the bubbles. The bubbles always drift to the surface. When you can't trust your feelings or judgment, you can always trust the bubbles to get you back to the top."

I have no intention of ever diving that deep and getting myself into that situation, but it's nice to know that I could always "feel the bubbles" as a reality check. Life is like scuba diving in that we need a way to determine what is real and true. Sometimes in life we get disoriented and desperate. At other times, we find ourselves drifting aimlessly. God knew that we would need instructions and examples about how to live. In the sixty-six books of the Bible, we have a reality library—stories, letters, guidelines, and examples from God that tell us what is true and real. In a world that is changing faster than we can imagine, we have something stable, true, and real. The Bible is our reality book, an amazing gift from God, who loves us deeply and desires a relationship with us.

A Closer Look—2 Timothy 3:16–17

God is the divine author of the Bible, choosing to work through many human authors over a period of time to give us his message. We use the word *inspiration* to describe God's work as the divine source of the Bible. The apostle Paul speaks of the divine inspiration of Scripture in 2 Timothy 3:16–17:

> [16]All Scripture is God-breathed [inspired] and is useful for teaching, rebuking, correcting and training in righteousness, [17]so that the man of God may be thoroughly equipped for every good work.

What Was Jesus' View of Scripture?
Do not think that I have come to abolish the Law or the Prophets; I have not come to abolish them but to fulfill them. I tell you the truth, until heaven and earth disappear, not the smallest letter, not the least stroke of a pen, will by any means disappear from the Law until everything is accomplished.
—Matthew 5:17–18

In 2 Timothy 3:16–17 the term "Scripture" refers specifically to the Old Testament. What does it refer to in 1 Timothy 5:18? How about 2 Peter 3:16?

Let's take a closer look at this text to get a better idea of what the Bible is and why God gave it to us.

Looking closely at a passage of Scripture is a lot like listening to another person—it takes time, concentration, and effort. The first step in listening to God's Word is understanding the passage's context, that is, the surrounding words, sentences, and paragraphs. Look up 2 Timothy in your Bible, and read the paragraph before and the paragraph after 3:16–17.

1. Who is writing this book, and to whom is he writing? (See 2 Tim. 1:1–2.)

2. In 3:10–13 Paul contrasts his way of life with the lifestyle of what group (see 3:1–9)?

3. What is Paul's specific command to Timothy in 3:14? What are the two reasons why Timothy should be motivated to continue in what he has learned (see 3:14–15)?

4. In 3:16 what are the two things that "Scripture is"?

Inspired by God

Paul says that Scripture is "God-breathed." What does this expression mean? Some versions translate the Greek word as "inspired," but the NIV has chosen "God-breathed"—a good translation. This is much more than saying that the Bible is inspiring, like a good movie or a romantic sunset. To say that the Bible is God-breathed, or inspired, is to say that it is God's Word. All Scripture, not just some of it, comes from the mouth of God. To read the Bible is to hear God speak, and what God speaks is completely true and reliable. What Scripture says, God says.

We are told that Scripture is both "God-breathed," or inspired, and useful or helpful. The order is important. Scripture is profitable and beneficial to us in life and ministry *because* it comes from God.

Profitable for Us

In the last part of verse 16 we are told that Scripture is useful or profitable for four things. What are those four things, and how do they relate to each other?

So Scripture comes from God and therefore proves helpful to us. But helpful in what sense? In 3:17 we find that the purpose of Scripture is accomplished in our lives when we read it and take it to heart. What is that purpose?

Summary

Let's say that you want to be a person of God who is "thoroughly equipped for every good work" (v. 17b). Summarize the advice given in 3:16–17 about how to become so equipped.

Jesus Believed the Bible

The first and foremost reason why Christians believe in the divine inspiration and authority of Scripture is . . . because of what Jesus Christ himself said. Since he endorsed the authority of Scripture, we are bound to conclude that his authority and Scripture's authority either stand or fall together. . . . All the available evidence confirms that Jesus Christ assented in his mind and submitted in his life to the authority of Old Testament Scripture. Is it not inconceivable that his followers should have a lower view of it than he?

—John Stott,
Authentic Christianity, 96

THE POWER OF WORDS

"teaching"—This word, frequently translated "doctrine," shows up often in Paul's letters to Timothy and Titus (1 Tim. 1:10; 4:1, 6, 13, 16; 5:17; 6:1, 3; 2 Tim. 3:16; 4:3; Titus 1:9; 2:1, 7, 10) and refers to reliable instruction in Christian belief and conduct. Scripture plays a primary role in equipping Christians in belief and behavior.

"rebuking"—This word refers to pointing out as well as refuting erroneous beliefs and practices.

"correcting"—This is the positive side to rebuking and deals with how to set everything right once the error has been identified. Scripture helps us restore or change our beliefs and practices.

"training in righteousness"—This phrase speaks of Scripture's role in helping us stay on the proper path through teaching and instruction in God's ways.

In 2 Timothy 3:14–4:2 Paul refers to the Scriptures in four ways. What are they?

The Primacy of Scripture

A writer and teacher who chose and ordered his words carefully, Mr. Lewis put "Scripture, the Church, Christian friends, books, etc." in this order by design. To him these avenues of revelation were not equal. Scripture, to Lewis, is the place where we hear God most clearly and definitively. Scripture is the litmus test of the validity of all other sources of Divine guidance. When the church, a book, or a Christian friend instructs in a way contradictory to the plenary meaning of the Bible, C. S. Lewis firmly dismissed the other voices.

—Lyle Dorsett,
Seeking the Secret Place, 52

Cross-References
Ps. 119; John 17:17; Rom. 15:4; Heb. 4:12; 2 Peter 1:20–21

For Deeper Study
Dockery, David S. *Christian Scripture.* Nashville: Broadman & Holman, 1995.
Marshall, I. Howard. *Biblical Inspiration.* Grand Rapids: Eerdmans, 1982.
Stott, John R. W. *Evangelical Truth: A Personal Plea for Unity, Integrity and Faithfulness.* Downers Grove, IL: InterVarsity Press, 1999.

So What?

1. Some people don't respect the Bible and deny its authority altogether. What other authority or authorities do they put in place of the Scriptures?

2. Sometimes those of us who hold to the authority of the Bible struggle to live out that belief in a consistent way. Would your friends and family say that your life demonstrates your belief in the authority of Scripture? What causes us to struggle to allow God's Word to have its rightful place of authority in our lives?

3. What is the best advice you have ever received about how to connect more consistently with God's Word?

4. What can you do this week to be more faithful to listening to God through his Word?

Handle with Care

Studying the Bible

If we really believe in the authority of the Bible, we will want to read it and study it on a regular basis. Some Christians, however, don't study the Word because they don't know how. They think the Bible is just for professionals or they feel intimidated or embarrassed by what they don't know. What you will learn in Behaving 1 will help you gain confidence in your ability to understand what God is saying to you through his Word. The experience of learning how to study the Scriptures will cultivate in you a firsthand faith, resulting in greater joy and excitement about following Jesus.

Studying the Bible is like taking a journey. Every time you open your Bible and read a passage, you are reading about people who lived and events that happened a long time ago. Yet because neither God's character nor human nature change, God's Word remains timeless and forever relevant. Don't worry, we don't bear the burden of having to make the Bible relevant; it is already relevant. We do, however, need to discover and explore how it relates to our lives. We need a reliable way to understand God's Word as it was intended. That's where the image of a journey proves helpful. (The journey image is taken from Scott Duvall and Daniel Hays, *Grasping God's Word*.) The "journey of the Bible" includes four steps:

1. *The meaning for the Biblical audience.* What did the passage mean to the biblical audience, to the people who first heard the words that we are now reading?
2. *The river of differences.* What are the differences and similarities between the biblical audience and us?

In your opinion, what are the top five reasons why people do not study the Bible?

1.

2.

3.

4.

5.

3. *The bridge of theological principles.* What are the timeless theological principles in the text that connect with both the biblical audience and with us?
4. *Contemporary application.* How can we apply that meaning to our lives today?

We begin our journey in the ancient world because that is where God first spoke his Word. If we ignore the ancient meaning, we will be tempted to make the Bible say what we want it to say, rather than discovering what it really says and means. We don't stay in the ancient world, since that wouldn't do us any good. Instead we cross into our world using a bridge built upon timeless, theological principles. Only then can we apply the meaning of the text to our lives. Let's look at each phase of the journey using 2 Timothy 2:15 as our example text. Open your Bible to 2 Timothy 2, and begin your journey.

1. The Meaning for the Biblical Audience

To grasp what the text meant to the biblical audience, you first need to understand the context. Read the verses before your passage as well as the verses that follow. What do you see in the surrounding context that helps you understand what Paul meant in verse 15?

We also need to find out about the historical situation that caused Paul to write to Timothy in the first place. A good study Bible (e.g., *The NIV Study Bible*) will tell you about the historical context of a book. Look in your study Bible at the beginning of both 1 and 2 Timothy and read about the author, setting, purpose, reasons for writing, and things like these. Is there anything in this information that helps you understand what Paul meant in 2:15?

After you get a feel for the context, look carefully at the passage itself. Circle important words, underline commands, bracket figures of speech, identify contrasts and comparisons, notice how significant nouns are described, be aware of the tone of the passage, and so on. Mark up the passage below with your observations. Don't worry about what it all means at this point, just look carefully at what it says.

Do your best to present yourself to God

as one approved, a workman

who does not need to be ashamed

and who correctly handles the word of truth.

Can you summarize what Paul meant when he wrote 2 Timothy 2:15?

What are the main traits of the false teaching that Timothy is fighting in Ephesus (see 2 Tim. 2:16–3:9)?

2. The River of Differences

Sometimes the river separating us from the biblical audience is narrow and shallow (e.g., James 1:19: "Everyone should be quick to listen, slow to speak and slow to become angry"). At other times, however, the river is wide and deep (e.g., 1 Cor. 11:4: "Every man who prays or prophesies with his head covered dishonors his head"). How does our situation differ from the circumstances Paul and Timothy faced?

How is our situation similar to theirs?

THE POWER OF WORDS

"correctly handles"—A metaphor that literally means "to cut straight." The background of the metaphor is unclear. It could refer to a stone mason making a straight cut, or to a farmer cutting a straight furrow, or to a person walking in a straight line. In any case, Paul is telling Timothy to handle the Christian message accurately, unlike the false teachers.

3. The Bridge of Theological Principles

We cross the bridge from the ancient world to our world by identifying theological truths that God intended to communicate through Paul to Timothy and the Ephesian church, and ultimately to us. This is the most challenging part of Bible study but also the most crucial for "handling the Word correctly." Write out a present-tense statement or principle that captures the heart of 2:15 by completing the following statement:

All Christians, but especially those church leaders responsible for the ministry of the Word, are supposed to . . .

This is your *theological principle*. Ask yourself the following questions to test the validity of the principle you have identified:

- Does your statement reflect what the Bible actually says and means?
- Is your statement relevant to both the ancient situation and the contemporary situation? A theological principle will be timeless and apply equally to both audiences.
- Is your statement consistent with the teaching of the rest of the Bible?

4. Contemporary Application

When you cross the bridge of theological principles, you are identifying the meaning of the text. We do not determine the meaning; we discover the meaning and then respond to that meaning. We refer to this response as "application." While the meaning of a passage never changes and is the same for all Christians, the application of that meaning may be different for every Christian. As you think about the context and meaning of 2 Timothy 2:15, what specific application is the Holy Spirit leading you to make part of your life? In other words, what particular changes does God want to make in your life related to how you handle the Bible?

So What?

1. Do you see a difference between reading the Bible and studying the Bible? Explain.

2. Are you really convinced deep down that you need to study the Bible? Why or why not?

3. What will happen over the long run if a person neglects (for whatever reason) the study of the Scriptures? What is your greatest struggle when it comes to Bible study?

4. Knowing that life change occurs in small increments ("little by little"), what one, small, realistic thing could you do this week to study God's Word more faithfully?

Cross-References
Ps. 119; Matt. 4:4; Acts 6:4; Col. 3:16; 1 Peter 2:1–2

For Deeper Study
Duvall, J. Scott, and J. Daniel Hays. *Grasping God's Word: A Hands-On Approach to Reading, Interpreting, and Applying the Bible.* 2nd ed. Grand Rapids: Zondervan, 2005.

Duvall, J. Scott, and J. Daniel Hays. *Journey into God's Word: Your Guide to Understanding and Applying the Bible.* Grand Rapids: Zondervan, 2007.

Fee, Gordon D., and Douglas Stuart. *How to Read the Bible for All Its Worth.* 3rd ed. Grand Rapids: Zondervan, 2003.

Hendricks, Howard G., and William D. Hendricks. *Living By the Book.* Revised and expanded. Chicago: Moody, 2007.

The Whole Truth and Nothing but the Truth

Truth

As what we believe and how we behave come together, they shape who we become. One quality that results from believing and studying the Bible is the quality of a truthful life. In our world truth is often considered an inconvenient liability rather than a godly asset, yet we know that God himself is the author of truth. If we want a meaningful relationship with the Lord, commitment to truth is not an option but a life essential. In fact, Jesus said, "I am the way and the truth and the life" (John 14:6). God is truth, and the closer we walk with him, the more truthful our lives will be. In Becoming 1 we will explore how we can live and speak truthfully in an age of exaggeration, spin, lies, and deceit.

We do indeed live in an age of spin. Bill Press, former host of CNN's *Crossfire*, attempts a definition:

There is no good definition of spin. It's easier to say what it's not than what it is: It's not the truth. Neither is it a lie. Spin lies somewhere in between: almost telling the truth, but not quite; bending the truth to make things look as good—or as bad—as possible; painting things in the best possible—or worst possible—light. (*Spin This*, xiv)

The first-century Roman world also had its share of spin doctors. The apostle Paul and other Christian teachers and missionaries had to distinguish themselves from popular preachers called Sophists who traveled around using their slick image and polished speaking ability to impress the crowds and pad their bank accounts. These swindlers would gladly twist the truth for personal profit. Paul does not hesitate to tell the churches that he and his coworkers would have nothing to do with such underhanded methods of spreading the gospel.

> Unlike so many, we do not peddle the word of God for profit. On the contrary, in Christ we speak before God with sincerity, like men sent from God. . . . Rather, we have renounced secret and shameful ways; we do not use deception, nor do we distort the word of God. On the contrary, by setting forth the truth plainly we commend ourselves to every man's conscience in the sight of God. (2 Cor. 2:17; 4:2)

> For the appeal we make does not spring from error or impure motives, nor are we trying to trick you. . . . You know we never used flattery, nor did we put on a mask to cover up greed—God is our witness. We were not looking for praise from men, not from you or anyone else. (1 Thess. 2:3, 5–6)

Clearly, truth twisting has always been a temptation for people living in a world where sin abounds. How, then, are Christians to live truthfully in a culture where falsehood is the norm?

A Closer Look—Ephesians 4:20–25

We see in Ephesians 4:20–25 a summary of Paul's advice on speaking and living truthfully.

[20]You, however, did not come to know Christ that way. [21]Surely you heard of him and were taught in him in accordance with the truth that is in Jesus. [22]You were taught, with regard to your former way of life, to put off your old self, which is being corrupted by its deceitful desires; [23]to be made new in the attitude of your minds; [24]and to put on the new self, created to be like God in true righteousness and holiness. [25]Therefore each of you must put off falsehood and speak truthfully to his neighbor, for we are all members of one body.

Wearing a Mask?

When people fail to live the truth they speak, we call them hypocrites. A hypocrite says one thing and does another. Our word *hypocrite* comes from the ancient Greek word *hypokritēs*. Classically, it denoted the actor in a drama who played a role on stage, often wearing a mask as part of a costume. In time *hypokritēs* came to have the negative connotation we associate with the English word *hypocrite*.

—Mark Roberts,
Dare to Be True, 143

The Old Testament has a lot to say about truth, often connecting it closely with faithfulness—a quality that fosters trust and makes relationships thrive. What do the following texts from Psalms teach us about truth?

- 15:1–2

- 40:11

- 43:3

- 51:6

- 86:11, 15

- 119:160

- 138:2

- 145:18

THE POWER OF WORDS

"falsehood"—The Greek word *pseudos* refers to a false statement or a lie, spoken with the intent to mislead or deceive. While God is the author of truth, Satan is the father of lies (John 8:44). Those who follow Jesus Christ are committed to truth (Rev. 14:5; 21:27), whereas those who are opposed to Christ prefer lies and deception (Rom. 1:25; 1 Tim. 4:1–2; Rev. 22:15).

1. To understand a text and apply its meaning to our lives, we always start with context. Read Ephesians 4:14–32 and note anything that helps you understand what Paul meant by the commands to "put off falsehood and speak truthfully" found in verse 25.

2. The word *however* in 4:20 indicates a contrast. What stands in contrast to the way the Ephesians came to know Christ? (What you win them with, you win them to!)

3. What is the basis or foundation of the command in 4:25 (see 4:21–24)? How does our identity in Christ relate to our experience of living truthfully?

4. Identify the negative command, the positive command, and the reason for the commands that Paul presents in 4:25. How do the two commands relate? Can you obey one without obeying the other?

Crossing the Bridge

Write a present-tense statement that captures the theological heart of Ephesians 4:25. Often in New Testament letters, the "river" separating us from the biblical audience is neither wide nor deep, so your statement may sound a lot like the verse.

As a way of validating the theological principle that you have just written, you can ask the following questions:

- Does your statement reflect what the text actually says and means?
- Is your statement relevant to both the ancient situation and the contemporary situation? A theological principle will be timeless and apply equally to both audiences.
- Is your statement consistent with the teaching of the rest of the Bible?

So What?

1. Have you ever been hurt by a lie (yours or someone else's)? Explain.

2. Why is lying a relationship killer?

3. Think about a recent situation where you were not completely honest. What pressured or motivated you to lie or spin the truth?

4. What helps you to recognize and to reject falsehood and deception?

Jesus said, "Simply let your 'Yes' be 'Yes,' and your 'No,' 'No'; anything beyond this comes from the evil one" (Matt. 5:37). What did he mean?

Growing Up

Then [as the church moves toward maturity] we will no longer be infants, tossed back and forth by the waves, and blown here and there by every wind of teaching and by the cunning and craftiness of men in their deceitful scheming. Instead, speaking the truth in love, we will in all things grow up into him who is the Head, that is, Christ.

—Ephesians 4:14–15

With reference to Eph. 4:15, which is the greater temptation for you, speaking (in love) something besides the truth or speaking the truth without love?

Cross-References
John 8:32; 14:6; 15:26; 16:13; 17:17; 2 Cor. 2:17; 4:2; Eph. 4:14–15; 6:14; Col. 3:9–10; 1 Thess. 2:3, 5–6; 1 John 2:21; 3:19–20; 5:20; 3 John 4

For Deeper Study
Baucham, Voddie. *The Ever-Loving Truth.* Nashville: Broadman & Holman, 2004.
Groothuis, Douglas. *Truth Decay.* Downers Grove, IL: InterVarsity Press, 2000.
Komp, Diane M. *Anatomy of a Lie: The Truth About Lies and Why Good People Tell Them.* Grand Rapids: Zondervan, 1998.
Lindsley, Art. *True Truth: Defending Absolute Truth in a Relativisitic World.* Downers Grove, IL: InterVarsity Press, 2004.
Matlock, Mark. *Don't Buy the Lie: Discerning Truth in a World of Deception.* Grand Rapids: Zondervan, 2004.
Roberts, Mark D. *Dare to Be True: Living in the Freedom of Complete Honesty.* Colorado Springs: Waterbrook, 2003.

5. Is there a person in your life who exemplifies truthful living? What would it take for you to be more like that person?

6. What specific steps can you take now to live more truthfully (e.g., Scripture memory, accountability partner, examining your motives)?

7. How can your Christian community promote truthfulness?

Three in One and One in Three

Triune God

For many people (some Christians included) the doctrine of the Trinity is about as exciting as doing advanced math blindfolded—overly complicated, boring, mysterious, and pointless. What difference does the obscure doctrine of God as Trinity really make after all? Why do we have to try to solve this theological puzzle? The simple answer is that this belief matters greatly if you want to know God and experience his salvation. Only God can save a person, and if God was not in Christ reconciling the world to himself (2 Cor. 5:19), then we cannot be in a right relationship with God. What sets Christianity apart from other religions is that we believe in one God who is Father, Son, and Spirit with each playing a unique role in rescuing lost humanity. In Believing 2, we will explore what it means to believe in the triune God revealed in Scripture. The relevance of this belief might surprise you.

The Oneness of God

The earliest Christians were Jews, and part of their Jewish heritage was a deeply held belief in the oneness of God (monotheism). The followers of the one God have always lived in a culture of multiple "gods"—the planets, the emperor, the inner self, wealth, or whatever. In sailing against the prevailing winds of polytheism (a belief in many gods), Christians followed the lead of their Master. For example, when asked about the greatest commandment, Jesus based his response on the oneness of God (Deut. 6:4–5):

> One of the teachers of the law came and heard them debating. Noticing that Jesus had given them a good answer, he asked him, "Of all the commandments, which is the most important?" "The most important one," answered Jesus, "is this: 'Hear, O Israel, the Lord our God, the Lord is one. Love the Lord your God with all your heart and with all your soul and with all your mind and with all your

strength.' The second is this: 'Love your neighbor as yourself.' There is no commandment greater than these." (Mark 12:28–31)

Along with this central passage from Deuteronomy, there are many other biblical texts that affirm that there is only one true God (e.g., Deut. 4:35, 39; 1 Kings 8:59–61; Isa. 43:10–11; Rom. 3:28–30; 1 Cor. 8:4, 6; 1 Tim. 1:17; 2:5; James 2:19).

The Deity of the Three

When we read the word *God* in the Bible, it normally refers to God the Father. Scripture clearly teaches that God the Father is divine. Based on the clear teaching of Scripture, Christians also believe that both Jesus Christ and the Holy Spirit are divine. Below you can read a few verses that teach the deity of both the Son and the Spirit.

> The high priest said to him, "I charge you under oath by the living God: Tell us if you are the Christ, the Son of God." "Yes, it is as you say," Jesus replied. (Matt. 26:63b–64a)

> In the beginning was the Word, and the Word was with God, and the Word was God. He was with God in the beginning. . . . The Word became flesh and made his dwelling among us. We have seen his glory, the glory of the One and Only, who came from the Father, full of grace and truth. (John 1:1–2, 14)

> [Jesus said,] "I and the Father are one." (John 10:30)

> Then Peter said, "Ananias, how is it that Satan has so filled your heart that you have lied to the Holy Spirit and have kept for yourself some of the money you received for the land? Didn't it belong to you before it was sold? And after it was sold, wasn't the money at your disposal? What made you think of doing such a thing? You have not lied to men but to God." (Acts 5:3–4)

> Don't you know that you yourselves are God's temple and that God's Spirit lives in you? If anyone destroys God's temple, God will destroy him; for God's temple is sacred, and you are that temple. (1 Cor. 3:16–17)

> Do you not know that your body is a temple of the Holy Spirit, who is in you, whom you have received from God? You are not your own; you were bought at a price. Therefore honor God with your body. (1 Cor. 6:19–20)

> In the past God spoke to our forefathers through the prophets at many times and in various ways, but in these last days he has spoken to us by his Son, whom he appointed heir of all things, and through whom he made the universe. The Son is the radiance of

God's glory and the exact representation of his being, sustaining all things by his powerful word. (Heb. 1:1–3a)

Triune God (Three-in-One)

The belief in God as Trinity comes from taking all of Scripture seriously. The Bible teaches God's oneness as well as the deity of Father, Son, and Spirit. There are not three separate Gods. There is only one God, but he always has and always will exist in three persons—Father, Son, and Spirit— all of whom are equally God. Thus, the "triune nature of God" refers to the one God in three persons.

There are a number of places in the Bible where the triune nature of God is captured in a verse or two. For example, Jesus teaches us to make disciples of all nations, "baptizing them in the name [singular] of the Father and of the Son and of the Holy Spirit" (Matt. 28:19). Speaking about the one God giving a variety of spiritual gifts, the apostle Paul says, "There are different kinds of gifts, but the same Spirit. There are different kinds of service, but the same Lord. There are different kinds of working, but the same God works all of them in all men" (1 Cor. 12:4–6). Paul also speaks of God's triune nature when encouraging the Corinthian Christians:

> Now it is *God* who makes both us and you stand firm in *Christ*. He anointed us, set his seal of ownership on us, and put his *Spirit* in our hearts as a deposit, guaranteeing what is to come. (2 Cor. 1:21–22)

> May the grace of the *Lord Jesus Christ*, and the love of *God*, and the fellowship of the *Holy Spirit* be with you all. (2 Cor. 13:14)

A Closer Look—Galatians 4:4–6

For our focal passage, let's look at Paul's encouraging words in Galatians 4:4–6. (Note: *Abba* is italic in NIV.)

The word **trinity** is never found in the Bible, but this does not mean that the concept of a triune God is absent from the Bible. Our beliefs are sometimes based on concepts that are bigger than single words.

Do you know of an analogy or two that can help you understand God as Trinity?

SCRIPTURE NOTES

⁴But when the time had fully come, *God* sent his *Son*, born of

a woman, born under law, ⁵to redeem those under law, that we

might receive the full rights of sons. ⁶Because you are sons,

God sent the *Spirit* of his *Son* into our hearts, the *Spirit* who

calls out, *"Abba, Father."*

Do you see any problems with analogies that help us understand God as Trinity?

1. Look up Galatians in your study Bible, and read about this letter. What are some of the main issues that Paul is confronting in his letter to the Galatians?

2. Read what comes before and after 4:4–6, and write down anything that helps you understand the context and meaning of this text.

3. Mark your observations of 4:4–6 below. Look for time references, lists, purpose statements, result statements, explanations, the actions of God, and so on.

But when the time had fully come,

God sent his Son, born of a woman,

born under law, to redeem those

under law, that we might receive

the full rights of sons. Because

you are sons, God sent the Spirit

of his Son into our hearts, the Spirit

who calls out, "Abba, Father."

4. How do you see the triune nature of God revealed in Galatians 4:4–6?

So What?

1. Groups that deny the doctrine of the Trinity have historically been considered cults. Why is believing in God as Trinity such a big deal? What would happen if you denied either the oneness of God or the deity of the Father, Son, or Spirit?

2. How do you personally experience each person of the Trinity?

3. Does viewing God as Trinity change your view of God in any way?

4. In some ways we can say that "God *is* community" (eternal three-in-one relationship of giving to others). What does God's being community say about the importance of fellowship or community for us?

Mutual Submission

The function of one member [person] of the Trinity may for a time be subordinate to one or both of the other members, but that does not mean he is in any way inferior in essence. Each of the three persons of the Trinity has had, for a period of time, a particular function unique to himself. This is to be understood as a temporary role for the purpose of accomplishing a given end, not a change in his status or essence.

—Millard J. Erickson,
Christian Theology, 338

Cross-References
Matt. 3:16–17; 28:19–20; John 1:33–34; 14:16, 26; 16:13–15; 20:21–22; Rom. 15:16; 1 Cor. 12:4–6; 2 Cor. 1:21–22; 13:14; Gal. 4:6; Rev. 1:4–5

For Deeper Study
Erickson, Millard J. *Christian Theology*. 2nd ed. Grand Rapids: Baker, 1998.
McGrath, Alister E. *Understanding the Trinity*. Grand Rapids: Zondervan, 1988.
Olson, Roger E. *The Mosaic of Christian Belief*. Downers Grove, IL: InterVarsity Press, 2002.
White, James R. *The Forgotten Trinity: Recovering the Heart of Christian Belief*. Minneapolis: Bethany House, 1998.

Life Together

Fellowshiping

Even if you and I (or any other human being) had never been born, God would still live in perfect community: Father, Son, and Spirit, three-in-one, one-in-three, living in eternal fellowship. Have you ever stopped to think about what that means for us? By making us in his image, God created in us a deep need for fellowship. As we experience the God who invented fellowship, we can expect him to draw us into deeper relationships with our friends in Christ. In Behaving 2 we will look at the habit of fellowship—living in authentic relationship with and dependence upon Jesus Christ and those who follow him.

Fellowship is both a *fact* of the Christian life and a *habit* or practice of the Christian life. It's like being a member of a family (fact) and then getting together with that family (habit), or being part of the church (fact) and then gathering with the church (habit). When it comes to fellowship, the fact or reality of fellowship makes possible the habit or practice.

Dietrich Bonhoeffer, the faithful German pastor who was hanged in a Nazi concentration camp just days before the Allies liberated the camp, wrote a classic book about fellowship called *Life Together.* He reminds us that fellowship is above all a new relationship we have with God and with other believers that is made possible by the death and resurrection of Jesus Christ and made personal and real by the presence of the Holy Spirit (2 Cor. 13:14; Phil. 2:1). Bonhoeffer stresses that "we belong to one another only through and in Jesus Christ" (*Life Together,* 21). There is no fellowship with God or with other Christians apart from Christ.

The apostle Paul says as much in 1 Corinthians 1:9—"God, who has called you into fellowship with his Son Jesus Christ our Lord, is faithful." John spells it out in even more detail:

The life [Jesus] appeared; we have seen it and testify to it, and we proclaim to you the eternal life, which was with the Father and has appeared to us. We proclaim to you what we have seen and heard, so that you also may have *fellowship* with us. And our *fellowship* is with the Father and with his Son, Jesus Christ. . . . This is the message we have heard from him and declare to you: God is light; in him there is no darkness at all. If we claim to have *fellowship* with him yet walk in the darkness, we lie and do not live by the truth. But if we walk in the light, as he is in the light, we have *fellowship* with one another, and the blood of Jesus, his Son, purifies us from all sin. (1 John 1:2–3, 5–7)

The New Testament uses different words to emphasize the fact or reality of fellowship. We are *partners* with other Christians in the cause of the gospel (Phil. 1:5; Philem. 17). We may even *participate* in the sufferings of Christ (Phil. 3:10; 1 Peter 4:13). As Christians, we refuse to *share* in the sins of others or *participate* with evil powers (1 Cor. 10:18, 20; 1 Tim. 5:22; 2 John 11).

The most noticeable fellowship habit in the New Testament is that of meeting practical needs. Christians living in authentic relationship with and dependence upon Jesus Christ will make it a priority to meet the needs of fellow Christians. The italicized words in the following verses are the English translations of Greek words for "fellowship":

Share with God's people who are in need. Practice hospitality. (Rom. 12:13)

For Macedonia and Achaia were pleased to make a *contribution* for the poor among the saints in Jerusalem. They were pleased to do it, and indeed they owe it to them. For if the Gentiles have *shared* in the Jews' spiritual blessings, they owe it to the Jews to *share* with them their material blessings. (Rom. 15:26–27)

For I testify that they gave as much as they were able, and even beyond their ability. Entirely on their own, they urgently pleaded with us for the privilege of *sharing* in this service to the saints. (2 Cor. 8:3–4)

Because of the service by which you have proved yourselves, men will praise God for the obedience that accompanies your confession of the gospel of Christ, and for your generosity in *sharing* with them and with everyone else. (2 Cor. 9:13)

Anyone who receives instruction in the word must *share* all good things with his instructor. (Gal. 6:6)

Moreover, as you Philippians know, in the early days of your acquaintance with the gospel, when I set out from Macedonia, not

---

Inspect Your Heart Before You Take the Lord's Supper?

You've probably heard preachers warn you to examine your heart carefully before you dare take the Lord's Supper based on Paul's warning to the Corinthian Christians:

> Therefore, whoever eats the bread or drinks the cup of the Lord in an unworthy manner will be guilty of sinning against the body and blood of the Lord. A man ought to examine himself before he eats of the bread and drinks of the cup. For anyone who eats and drinks without recognizing the body of the Lord eats and drinks judgment on himself. (1 Cor. 11:27–29)

The best of evangelical scholarship suggests that some Corinthians were sinning by failing to use their material resources to meet the practical needs of others in their church. They were failing at fellowship. Craig Blomberg writes,

> Many Christians have entirely missed the real meaning of these threats, which, . . . are directed against those who are not adequately loving their Christian brothers and sisters and providing for their physical or material needs. . . . [Paul's] warning was not to those who were leading unworthy lives and longed for forgiveness. . . . [Rather, his warning was this]—Those who eat and drink in flagrant disregard of the physical needs of others in their fellowship risk incurring the punishment of God. (*1 Corinthians*, 231–33)

God is very concerned with how his children treat each other, and not even the Lord's Supper can be used as an excuse to neglect each other's needs.

"apostles' teaching"—This phrase probably refers to the teachings of Jesus passed down through his apostles. These teachings likely focused on the life, ministry, teachings, death, and resurrection of Jesus, along with the response to this good news and the Spirit's work through the church. Today this authoritative teaching is accessible in the New Testament.

"fellowship"—In the New Testament period, the word *koinōnia* (fellowship) was used of business partnerships in which people were connected through work. It was also a favorite expression to describe the marriage relationship. The basic idea of the word involves generosity in sharing, giving, or participating.

"breaking of bread"—This expression probably has a double significance. First, it refers to sharing a meal in a home. Second, it also refers to the Christian practice of taking the Lord's Supper as part of that ordinary fellowship meal.

one church *shared* with me in the matter of giving and receiving, except you only; for even when I was in Thessalonica, you sent me aid again and again when I was in need. (Phil. 4:15–16)

Command those who are rich in this present world not to be arrogant nor to put their hope in wealth, which is so uncertain, but to put their hope in God, who richly provides us with everything for our enjoyment. Command them to do good, to be rich in good deeds, and to be generous and *willing to share*. (1 Tim. 6:17–18)

And do not forget to do good and to *share* with others, for with such sacrifices God is pleased. (Heb. 13:16)

Kent Hughes helps us to see that the biblical reality of fellowship always involves giving:

Fellowship is not just a sentimental feeling of oneness. It is not punch and cookies. It does not take place simply because we are in the church ["fellowship"] hall. Fellowship comes through *giving*. True fellowship costs! So many people never know the joys of Christian fellowship because they have never learned to give themselves away. . . . Do you want to have fellowship? You must be a giver. (*Acts: The Church Afire*, 49)

A Closer Look—Acts 2:42–47

The first two chapters of Acts are packed with unusual and exciting information about the early church. The final paragraph of chapter 2 sums up the condition of the church in those very early days and makes it clear that fellowship was at the heart of the life of the early church.

> [42]They [the church] devoted themselves to the apostles' teaching and to the fellowship, to the breaking of bread and to prayer. [43]Everyone was filled with awe, and many wonders and miraculous signs were done by the apostles. [44]All the believers were together and had everything in common. [45]Selling their possessions and goods, they gave to anyone as he had need. [46]Every day they continued to meet together in the temple courts. They broke bread in their homes and ate together with

glad and sincere hearts, [47]praising God and enjoying the favor

of all the people. And the Lord added to their number daily

those who were being saved.

The questions below may help you grasp the meaning of Acts 2:42–47.

1. Those first Christians devoted themselves to four things (v. 42). What were they?

2. What would be the contemporary equivalent of these four things? (See "The Power of Words" for help.)

3. Not everything in 2:43–47 relates to fellowship, but much of it does. What do you see in the rest of this paragraph that helps you understand how the first Christians experienced true fellowship?

Crossing the Bridge

How does our situation differ from the early church situation described in Acts 2:42–47?

- We cannot meet together in the temple courts (v. 46).

-

-

Community and Solitude

Let him who cannot be alone beware of community. He will only do harm to himself and to the community. Alone you stood before God when he called you; alone you had to answer that call; alone you had to struggle and pray; and alone you will die and give an account to God. You cannot escape from yourself; for God singled you out. . . .

But the reverse is also true: *Let him who is not in community beware of being alone.* Into the community you were called, the call was not meant for you alone; in the community of the called you bear your cross, you struggle, you pray. You are not alone, even in death, and on the Last Day you will be only one member of the great congregation of Jesus Christ.

We recognize, then, that only as we are within the fellowship can we be alone, and only he that is alone can live in the fellowship.

—Dietrich Bonhoeffer,
Life Together, 77

Cross-References

Look back over the references cited throughout Behaving 2.

For Deeper Study

Bolinger, Tod E. *It Takes a Church to Raise a Christian*. Grand Rapids: Brazos, 2004.

Bonhoeffer, Dietrich. *Life Together*. San Francisco: HarperSanFrancisco, 1954.

Ortberg, John. *Everybody's Normal Till You Get to Know Them*. Grand Rapids: Zondervan, 2003.

Wilson, Jonathan R. *Why Church Matters: Worship, Ministry, and Mission in Practice*. Grand Rapids: Brazos, 2006.

What theological principles do you see in Acts 2:42–47 that tell us what fellowship is and how we can experience it? (Remember, theological principles should apply equally well to the biblical audience and to us.)

- We can be together and not experience fellowship, but we can't experience fellowship if we do not spend time together (principle from v. 44).

-

-

So What?

1. How does fellowship relate to friendship?

2. When you are with other Christians, what do you spend time doing?

3. How much time do you spend with other Christians devoting yourselves to the study of the Bible, to prayer, to community building, to meeting practical needs, and to worship?

4. Do you know anybody in your church with financial or other practical needs? How would you ever find out if people had such needs in our society?

5. What are some ways that God might be calling you to use your time and money to meet the practical needs of other Christians?

6. Do you personally have practical needs that your community group could meet?

The Greatest of These

Love

God is Trinity—Father, Son, and Spirit living in an eternal relationship of self-giving love. God wants us to experience this community of love with him. We need him, and we need each other. We've seen how fellowship is both a reality we enter into when we are joined to Christ and a habit of giving to other believers. When we accept God's invitation to join his community, we begin to open our hearts and hands and let his love flow through us to meet the practical needs of others. When we become passionately consumed with giving to others and doing what God says is best for them, our lives will be characterized by love. In Becoming 2 we will look at the character quality of love, the king of the virtues—"the greatest of these."

Love is what holds us together in the messy, nitty-gritty of life as a community. We sometimes enter a community with our own dream or vision of what that community should be like. Then we meet that irritating person, or things don't go our way, or the decision is made without us, or something else happens that challenges our perfect ideal of community. God begins to shatter our dream and our ideal and replace it with his reality and truth. At that point we have a choice to make—either we hand over our dreams to God, or we continue to fight for our own vision of community. Dietrich Bonhoeffer offers a sobering warning about this important choice:

> Every human wish dream that is injected into the Christian community is a hindrance to genuine community and must be banished if genuine community is to survive. He who loves his dream of a community more than the Christian community itself becomes a

What is the difference between being un-
loved and being unlovable?

?

Love Takes a Risk

To love at all is to be vulnerable. Love
anything, and your heart will certainly
be wrung and possibly be broken. If you
want to make sure of keeping it intact,
you must give your heart to no one, not
even to an animal. . . . The only place
outside Heaven where you can be per-
fectly safe from all the dangers . . . of
love is Hell.

—C. S. Lewis,
The Four Loves, 111–12

destroyer of the latter, even though his personal intentions may be
ever so honest and earnest and sacrificial. (*Life Together*, 27)

What is your vision, or "wish dream," for your community? Are you
willing to sacrifice your dream so that God may give you his dream?

The Bible speaks often about love (see the many cross-references on
page 47). In 1 Corinthians 13:4–7 the apostle Paul defines what biblical love
is and what it is not:

Love is patient, love is kind. It does not envy, it does not boast, it is
not proud. It is not rude, it is not self-seeking, it is not easily angered,
it keeps no record of wrongs. Love does not delight in evil but
rejoices with the truth. It always protects, always trusts, always
hopes, always perseveres.

In the original language Paul uses fifteen verbs in this passage to define
love. Instead of "love is patient" or "love is kind," the idea is more like "love
acts with patience" or "love shows kindness." Love is an action before it is
an emotion. This means that we can love people we don't even like. The
story below reminds us that love is primarily a choice.

Newspaper columnist and minister George Crane tells of a wife
who came into his office full of hatred toward her husband. "I do
not only want to get rid of him; I want to get even. Before I divorce
him, I want to hurt him as much as he has me." Dr. Crane suggested
an ingenious plan. "Go home and act as if you really loved your
husband. Tell him how much he means to you. Praise him for every
decent trait. Go out of your way to be as kind, considerate, and
generous as possible. Spare no efforts to please him, to enjoy him.
Make him believe that you love him. After you've convinced him of
your undying love and that you cannot live without him, then drop
the bomb. Tell him that you're getting a divorce. That will really
hurt him." With revenge in her eyes, she smiled and exclaimed,
"Beautiful, beautiful. Will he ever be surprised!" And she did it
with enthusiasm. Acting "as if." For two months she showed love,
kindness, listening, giving, reinforcing, sharing. When she didn't
return, Crane called. "Are you ready now to go through with the
divorce?" "Divorce!" she exclaimed. "Never! I discovered I really do
love him." Her actions had changed her feelings. Motion resulted in
emotion. The ability to love is established not so much by fervent
promise as often repeated deeds. (Larson, *Illustrations*, 137)

Love is a choice to do what God says is best for another person.

Only God's love flowing through us will keep us bound together in fellowship. Yet there is a lot of confusion about what love really means, even

among Christians. What are some common ways our culture defines "love" that are different from the Bible's definition?

Jesus' Final Words
On the night before he was crucified, Jesus talked a lot about love. People usually don't waste words right before they die. Read John 13–15 and summarize what Jesus is teaching us about love.

A Closer Look—1 John 4:7–8

Our focal passage in this study is 1 John 4:7–8. Mark up the passage below with your observations. Look for important words, commands, contrasts, purpose statements, result statements, pronouns, conjunctions, emotional terms, and so on.

SCRIPTURE NOTES

7aBeloved, let us love one another,

7bfor love is from God;

7cand everyone who loves is born of God and knows God.

8aThe one who does not love does not know God,

8bfor God is love. (NASB)

1. Look at the context of the text. Begin by reading the introduction to 1 John in a study Bible. Why does John emphasize the theme of love in this letter?

2. Since a new section probably starts at verse 7, the immediate context of our passage is 4:7–12. Read these verses, and jot down what they teach us about love.

   • 4:7–8

   • 4:9–10

   • 4:11–12

Letting God Love Us
I will love God because he first loved me. I will obey God because I love God. But if I cannot accept God's love, I cannot love him in return, and I cannot obey him. Self-discipline will never make us feel righteous or clean; accepting God's love will.

—Don Miller,
Blue Like Jazz, 86

Write your favorite quote about biblical love:

3. What is the key command (v. 7a)?

4. What are the two reasons that we should obey the command (vv. 7b, 8b)?

5. When the Bible says that "God is love" (v. 8b), is that the same as saying that "love is God"? What does "God is love" mean?

6. What is the result of carrying out the command? The result is stated both positively (4:7c) and negatively (4:8a).

7. Why does John say "knows God" rather than "knows about God"?

Crossing the Bridge

Write a present-tense statement that captures the theological heart of 1 John 4:7–8. In this case the "river" separating us from the biblical audience is neither wide nor deep.

So What?

1. What is the most important thing God seems to be saying to you through 1 John 4:7–8?

2. In your own words, explain the connection between Trinity, fellowshiping (or community), and love.

3. Who is the most loving human being you know? What are some specific things that person has done to show love to you and to others?

4. What is the difference between saying "Emily is loving" and "God is love"?

5. What are the greatest obstacles to love in your life?

6. What are three specific things you can do this week to cultivate biblical love in your life?

Cross-References (a partial list)
Matt. 5:44; Luke 10:25–37; John 3:16; 13:34–35; 14:15, 21, 23; 15:9–10; 21:15–17; Rom. 5:5, 8; 8:31–39; 12:9; 13:8–10; 1 Cor. 13; Gal. 5:13–15, 22; Eph. 3:14–19; 5:1–2; Col. 3:14; 1 Peter 4:8; 1 John 3:11–18; 4:7–21

For Deeper Study
Lewis, C. S. *The Four Loves.* Glasgow: William Collins, 1960.
Ortberg, John. *Love Beyond Reason: Moving God's Love from Your Head to Your Heart.* Grand Rapids: Zondervan, 1998.
Smedes, Lewis B. *Love Within Limits.* Grand Rapids: Eerdmans, 1978.
Yancey, Philip. *What's So Amazing About Grace?* Grand Rapids: Zondervan, 1997.

Our Father in Heaven

Great and Good God

Growing up Baptist, our mealtime prayers were short, sweet, and rarely the same. The adults in my circle sometimes fell into prayer ruts, and those ruts normally focused on food as much as on God—"Bless this food to the nourishment of our bodies and our bodies to Thy service." In contrast, the mealtime prayers of my liturgical Lutheran cousins were always the same—"God is great, God is good, let us thank him for our food. Amen." As a child in one faith tradition listening to the prayers of children in another tradition, their single mealtime prayer seemed repetitive, boring, and meaningless. Repetitive—yes; boring—maybe; but meaningless—never. This simple childhood prayer captures the very heart of what Christians have always believed about who God is.

God Is Great

Christians claim that God is both great and good. On the one hand, God is great, transcendent (far removed), holy, infinite, powerful, majestic, sovereign, and independent. Many, many passages of Scripture confirm God's greatness. Here are just a few:

> Who among the gods is like you, O Lord? Who is like you—majestic in holiness, awesome in glory, working wonders? (Exod. 15:11)

> I am the Lord who brought you up out of Egypt to be your God; therefore be holy, because I am holy. (Lev. 11:45)

> With man this is impossible, but not with God; all things are possible with God. (Mark 10:27)

> The God who made the world and everything in it is the Lord of heaven and earth and does not live in temples built by hands. And he is not served by human hands, as if he needed anything, because he himself gives all men life and breath and everything else. (Acts 17:24–25)

Nothing in all creation is hidden from God's sight. Everything is uncovered and laid bare before the eyes of him to whom we must give account. (Heb. 4:13)

God Is Good

On the other hand, God is good, imminent (close or near), loving, gracious, merciful, compassionate, self-sacrificing, kind, and faithful. He is not an impersonal force, but a person who invites us into an intimate relationship. Scripture also affirms God's goodness:

Know therefore that the LORD your God is God; he is the faithful God, keeping his covenant of love to a thousand generations of those who love him and keep his commands." (Deut. 7:9)

But you, O Lord, are a compassionate and gracious God, slow to anger, abounding in love and faithfulness. (Ps. 86:15)

Give thanks to the LORD, for he is good. His love endures forever. (Ps. 136:1)

The God revealed to us in the Bible is both great and good. Since *God is great,* he can do something about the suffering and evil in the world. He can rescue people from their sins. He can answer prayer, perform miracles, and bring about a final victory over evil.

Since *God is good,* he gets involved in a personal way with his creation. He is available and near. He enters into a covenant relationship with us, understands our weaknesses, and responds compassionately to our needs.

A Closer Look—Matthew 6:9

At the very center of Jesus' Sermon on the Mount stands the "Lord's Prayer" (Matt. 6:9–15). The prayer begins very simply, "Our Father in heaven." This brief expression summarizes God's character as a great and good God.

Our Father

Throughout the Old Testament, God is portrayed as the "Father" of Israel— "When Israel was a child, I loved him, and out of Egypt I called my son" (Hos. 11:1). It was rare, however, to find individual Israelites addressing God as "Father." God was the Father of the nation.

When Jesus arrived on the scene, he made the bold claim that God was his Father—"All things have been handed over to Me by My Father; and no one knows the Son except the Father; nor does anyone know the Father except the Son, and anyone to whom the Son wills to reveal Him" (Matt. 11:27 NASB). Jesus used the expression "My Father" as his primary way of addressing God. Jesus never referred to "our Father" (in Matthew 6:9 he is teaching *us* how to pray) since his sonship is absolutely unique and different

Notice what happens when we deny either God's greatness or his goodness:

Deism—A view of God that portrays him as creating the world but then not getting involved with the world. He is the designer of the universe but not intimately or personally involved with his creation. The deist god may be compared to an absentee landlord. He started the project and then abandoned it. The deist god doesn't answer prayer, perform miracles, or relate personally with his creation. He is great but not good.

Panentheism—A view of God that overemphasizes God's goodness to the neglect of his greatness. God and the world are not identical, but God is dependent on the world. Without the world, God could not be God, according to this view. The panentheist god is always in the process of becoming god. He is the fellow sufferer who loves, cares, and understands, but he is not sovereign, in control, or all-powerful. God is good but not great.

I will exalt you, my God the King; I will praise your name for ever and ever. Every day I will praise you and extol your name for ever and ever. Great is the LORD and most worthy of praise; his greatness no one can fathom. One generation will commend your works to another; they will tell of your mighty acts. They will speak of the glorious splendor of your majesty, and I will meditate on your wonderful works. They will tell of the power of your awesome works, and I will proclaim your great deeds. They will celebrate your abundant goodness and joyfully sing of your righteousness. The LORD is gracious and compassionate, slow to anger and rich in love. The LORD is good to all; he has compassion on all he has made. All you have made will praise you, O LORD; your saints will extol you. They will tell of the glory of your kingdom and speak of your might, so that all men may know of your mighty acts and the glorious splendor of your kingdom. Your kingdom is an everlasting kingdom, and your dominion endures through all generations. The LORD is faithful to all his promises and loving toward all he has made. The LORD upholds all those who fall and lifts up all who are bowed down. The eyes of all look to you, and you give them their food at the proper time. You open your hand and satisfy the desires of every living thing. The LORD is righteous in all his ways and loving toward all he has made. The LORD is near to all who call on him, to all who call on him in truth. He fulfills the desires of those who fear him; he hears their cry and saves them. The LORD watches over all who love him, but all the wicked he will destroy. My mouth will speak in praise of the LORD. Let every creature praise his holy name for ever and ever.

from ours. Jesus is the Son by nature; we are sons and daughters by adoption. He is the Son by right; we are sons and daughters by grace. He says "My Father"; we say "our Father." What is amazing is that Jesus teaches his disciples to call God "Father." As adopted children, we cry "Abba! Father!"

> For you did not receive a spirit that makes you a slave again to fear, but you received the Spirit of sonship. And by him we cry, *"Abba, Father."* The Spirit himself testifies with our spirit that we are God's children. (Rom. 8:15–16)

What does it mean to you that Jesus instructs you to call God "Father"?

The title "Father" indicates that God desires an intimate, personal relationship with you. God's goodness and tenderness come through when Jesus gives you permission to address God in this way.

Frederick Bruner helps us see this even more clearly:

> The "our" [in "Our Father"] means belonging, mercy, home. It is a *possessive* pronoun meaning that God the Father is ours and we are his. In the "our" is contained the joy of the whole gospel. We will never be able to calculate the honor that has been done us by being allowed to pray "Our Father." (*Christbook*, 239)

Think a bit more about what our Father does for us:

- Our Father rewards us for "secret service" (Matt. 6:3–4, 6, 17–18)
- Our Father knows what we need before we ask him (Matt. 6:8)
- Our Father will meet our needs (Matt. 6:32–34)
- Our Father has prepared an inheritance for us (Matt. 25:34; Col. 1:12)
- Our Father is merciful (Luke 6:36)
- Our Father loves us, whether we are unrighteous or self-righteous (Luke 15:11–32)
- Our Father seeks our worship (John 4:23–24)
- Our Father protects us from spiritual harm (John 10:29; 17:11)
- Our Father comforts us (2 Cor. 1:3–4)
- Our Father has given us the Holy Spirit (John 14:16, 26; Gal. 4:4–6)
- Our Father has blessed us with every spiritual blessing in Christ (Eph. 1:3)
- Our Father has given us new life (1 Peter 1:3)
- Our Father loves us (1 John 3:1)

In Heaven

God is not only "Our Father," he is our Father "in heaven." We tend to become too familiar with God in our culture. God is often addressed in ways that are informal to the point of being irreverent. You have probably heard that the Aramaic word *abba* meant "Daddy." In the 1960s a scholar named Joachim Jeremias popularized this view, but his scholarship was flawed. Later, after being corrected by other scholars, Jeremias himself admitted his mistake, but not before preachers had picked up the idea that *abba* was a child's tender word for daddy and encouraged us to call God "Daddy." The word *abba* was used by children, but it was also used by adults to speak to their fathers. "Abba" (which isn't used in the Lord's Prayer) simply means father and should be translated "Father," not "Daddy." Jesus teaches us that real prayer begins with a respectful awe of the Lord.

Just because God is good and wants an intimate relationship with us doesn't mean that we should lose sight of his greatness. He is our Father "in heaven." He is high and lifted up. He is the almighty Creator of heaven and earth. He is the sovereign King of the universe. To him belongs all glory and honor and power. He is seated on the throne of heaven, and we should approach him with awe and reverence.

What can you do to deepen your reverence for God?

Great prayers reveal a great awareness of God. Jesus teaches us to pray, "Our Father in heaven." God desires an intimate, personal relationship with us because he is "our Father" and he has adopted us in Christ. Because he is our Father "in heaven," we bow before him in humility and respect. The childhood mealtime prayer of my Lutheran cousins got it right. God is both great and good. When we have a biblical, balanced view of God's nature as both great and good, we will want to thank him for our food, for our lives, for everything. We call that worship, and that is the habit that flows out of trusting in our great and good God.

Adoption

We biological parents know well the earnest longing to have a child. But in many cases our cribs were filled easily. We decided to have a child and a child came.... I've heard of unplanned pregnancies, but I've never heard of an unplanned adoption. That's why adoptive parents understand God's passion to adopt us. They know what it means to feel an empty space inside. They know what it means to hunt, to set out on a mission, and take responsibility for a child with a spotted past and a dubious future. If anybody understands God's ardor for his children, it's someone who has rescued an orphan from despair, for that is what God has done for us. God has adopted you. God sought you, found you, signed the papers and took you home.

—Max Lucado,
The Great House of God, 15

Cross-References (a partial list)
Job 38:1–42:6; Psalm 23; 89; 104; 107; Isa. 6:1–7; Matt. 5:48; Mark 14:35–36; Rom. 8:15–16; 2 Cor. 1:3–4; Gal. 4:6; Heb. 12:3–11; Rev. 4–5

For Deeper Study

Carson, D. A. *The Sermon on the Mount: An Evangelical Exposition of Matthew 5–7.* Grand Rapids: Baker, 1978.

Dodd, Brian J. *Praying Jesus' Way.* Downers Grove, IL: InterVarsity Press, 1997.

Lucado, Max. *The Great House of God.* Dallas: Word, 1997.

Olson, Roger E. *The Mosaic of Christian Belief.* Downers Grove, IL: InterVarsity Press, 2002.

So What?

1. What is the most dominant picture of God in your mind? A grandfather? An authority figure? A best friend?

2. In what ways has your relationship with your earthly parents shaped your view of God?

3. More than anything else, what helps you sense that God wants to draw you close and enjoy an intimate relationship with you as your loving Father?

4. On the other hand, what helps you recognize and stand in awe of God's holiness, mighty power, and glorious majesty?

5. Are you drawn more to God's greatness or goodness? What do you need to do to move toward a more balanced understanding of God as both great and good?

Come, Let Us Bow Down

Worshiping

"God is great, God is good, let us thank him . . ." This children's prayer confesses God's character as holy, majestic, and powerful but also as loving, gracious, and merciful. While God is enthroned on high as the sovereign Creator of the universe, he is also our Father, who knows us by name and longs for our companionship. The unapproachable Light has chosen to come near as our Friend. The belief that God is both great and good leads us to respond with praise, gratitude, and obedience. In other words, when we see ourselves for who we are and God for who he is, we bow down. In Behaving 3, we will take a closer look at the habit of Christian worship—the one thing we were all created for.

High and lofty realities are hard to define because they resist being reduced to a few words. Worship falls into that category. We should try to define worship (see Louie Giglio's helpful definition on page 56), but we shouldn't be surprised if our attempts fall short. In fact, describing worship is often more helpful than trying to define it. For instance, authentic Christian worship . . .

- never starts with us. God begins worship by creating us, loving us, and blessing us. Everything we do in worship begins with God.
- is our response to God for who he is and what he has done. This involves praise, thanksgiving, gratitude, reverence, and many other things.
- is holistic, involving all of us (i.e., what we think, say, and do) in all of life, not just on Sunday mornings.

**"Sing to the Lord a New Song"
(Pss. 93–100)**

Take time this week to read these magnificent psalms of worship. As you read and reflect on these psalms, consider . . .

- What is God like?
- What has God done for you?
- How are we supposed to respond to God?
- How is God calling us to worship him?

SCRIPTURE NOTES

- is both personal and corporate. Our worship will never be complete unless we connect with a local body of believers to honor and exalt the Lord together.
- includes obedience. Gathering with other believers is just one aspect of offering ourselves to God as living, holy, and pleasing sacrifices.

Even better than defining or describing worship is experiencing worship. If you want to grow and mature in this habit, you need to connect with a local church and participate in corporate worship. What should you look for when trying to find a community that worships biblically? The New Testament consistently identifies six essential elements of Christian worship:

- Praise (Eph. 5:18–20; Col. 3:16)
- Prayers (Acts 2:42; 4:24; 1 Tim. 2:1–2; James 5:16)
- Scripture reading (Col. 4:16; 1 Thess. 5:27; 1 Tim. 4:13)
- Teaching and exhortation from Scripture (2 Tim. 4:1–4; Tit. 2:15; Heb. 10:24–25)
- Giving an offering (1 Cor. 16:1–2; 2 Cor. 8:1–8; 9:6–13)
- Baptism and the Lord's Supper (ordinances) (Matt. 26:26–29; 28:18–20; Acts 2:38–41; 1 Cor. 11:20–34)

All six elements are extremely significant and serve to enrich our personal encounter with God, but unless his Spirit touches our spirit, we have not truly worshiped (see the Foster quote on page 56).

A Closer Look—Psalm 100

Our focal passage in this study is Psalm 100.

[1]Shout for joy to the LORD, all the earth.

[2]Worship the LORD with gladness; come before him with joyful songs.

[3]Know that the LORD is God. It is he who made us, and we are his;

we are his people, the sheep of his pasture.

[4]Enter his gates with thanksgiving and his courts with praise;

give thanks to him and praise his name.

[5]For the LORD is good and his love endures forever;

his faithfulness continues through all generations.

Psalm 100 serves as the dramatic conclusion to a series of hymns celebrating God's greatness and goodness (93–99). This hymn was sung during one of the Jewish festivals as people gathered to recognize God as King over all the earth. Use the questions below to dig deeper into Psalm 100.

1. What are the seven commands in verses 1–4?

2. What is the central command (v. 3)? Why is this command foundational to the other six commands? (Hint: Look carefully at the explanation in v. 3b.)

3. What are the attitudes or actions of worship (e.g., "with gladness" or "with praise")?

4. What are the reasons for worship (see v. 5)?

5. What does this psalm tell us about who we are? What does it tell us about who God is? How does true worship connect these two?

Crossing the Bridge

What are the differences between the biblical audience and us? For example, when we gather for worship, we don't enter the gates or courts of the Old Testament temple. Do you notice any other differences?

Making the Most of Corporate Worship

Worship is much more than just gathering with other Christians to pray, give money, sing praises, hear scriptural teaching, and celebrate baptism and the Lord's Supper. Worship is a relational encounter with God rather than a set of religious rituals. If we never let God break through to us, we will find it difficult to respond to him. Think about the priority you place on corporate worship.

How do you prepare for worship?

What hinders you from worshiping?

Where does corporate worship rank in priority right now in your life?

For Deeper Study

Beach, Nancy. *An Hour on Sunday: Creating Moments of Transformation and Wonder.* Grand Rapids: Zondervan, 2004.

Foster, Richard J. *Celebration of Discipline.* 25th anniversary ed. San Francisco: HarperSanFrancisco, 2003.

Giglio, Louie. *The Air I Breathe: Worship as a Way of Life.* Sisters, OR: Multnomah, 2003.

Peterson, David. *Engaging with God: A Biblical Theology of Worship.* Downers Grove, IL: InterVarsity Press, 1992.

Rognlien, Bob. *Experiential Worship: Encountering God with Heart, Soul, Mind and Strength.* Colorado Springs: NavPress, 2005.

What are the timeless theological principles in Psalm 100 that connect with both the biblical audience and with us (the bridge between their time and ours)?

So What?

1. What is your favorite definition of worship?

2. Which New Testament elements of worship does your local church emphasize the most? Which ones would you like to emphasize more in corporate worship?

3. What have been some of your most memorable corporate worship experiences?

4. How important are worship forms or styles to you? Why?

5. What do you need to do to deepen your worship of the great and good God?

6. What are two specific ways that you can live out the message of Psalm 100 this week?

Be Holy, Because
I Am Holy

Purity

The belief that God is both great and good—"our Father in heaven"—calls for the only appropriate response to God's "overture of love"—the habit of worship. Worship is "our response, both personal and corporate, to God—for who He is and what He has done expressed in and by the things we say and the way we live" (Louie Giglio, *The Air I Breathe*, 49). Our response should be more than a Sunday morning, lifting-voices, raising-hands, praying-prayers response. Gathering with other believers to worship is crucial to a healthy spiritual life, but we worship primarily by how we live. The habit of whole-life worship nurtures in us the character quality of purity—living a holy life in public and private that honors God.

In the spring of 1995, revival broke out on many college campuses across America. One characteristic of this visitation from God was students dealing with sinful habits that they had previously let linger in their lives. Bonne Steffen interviewed several students for *The Christian Reader*. One student named Brian at Asbury College said,

I was a leader on campus. We had invited Wheaton students to come and share. At first, I was praying for other people, but then I began to think about my own struggles. I stood in line for three hours with one of my best friends all the time thinking, *How can I get up there and admit I'm less than perfect?* But I also realized that being on a Christian campus isn't protection from the world. I have really struggled with lust. I found I wasn't alone. It was an issue for a lot of others. Personally, I wanted the chain to be broken; I wanted that stuff out of my life. If it meant no magazines, no television, I was willing to eliminate them. A number of us signed a paper stating our desire for purity, which we put in a box and placed on the altar. I'm still accountable to other people. My deepest desire is to be pure in my heart and thoughts. (Larson, *Choice Contemporary Stories*, 217)

Brian was busy serving God as a ministry leader but was not ready to admit he needed God's help in his own life. He discovered, however, that God cares as much about his character as his ministry. What was the turning point for Brian?

Things begin to happen in our lives when it dawns on us that God cares as much about *working in* our lives as he does about *working through* our lives.

Be Holy?

God is utterly pure and perfect. He is distinct and separate from everything he created and all other competing gods. We need a word to describe how God's very being is different from anything we know—our word is *holy*. In other words, God defines holiness; it is not the other way around. (By the way, the words translated "pure" and "holy" in our New Testaments come from the same word family in Greek.)

A common name for God in the Old Testament is the "Holy One" (Isa. 40:25; 43:15; Ezek. 39:7; Hos. 11:9). People, places, and things are "holy" only because they are in contact with God, who alone is holy. That closeness to God explains why in the Old Testament the tabernacle and temple are considered holy. That connection also helps us understand why a common New Testament description for those who belong to God is "holy ones" (normally translated "saints"). God's people are holy because they belong to God, are connected to God, and are close to God.

When we enter a relationship with God through Jesus Christ, we are given God's Holy Spirit, and our physical bodies become the temple of the Holy Spirit (1 Cor. 6:19). In this sense, we have already become holy (i.e., indwelt by the Holy Spirit). God then has every right to command us to act holy.

A Closer Look—1 Peter 1:13–16

Let's focus in this study on 1 Peter 1:13–16. Beginning in 1:13 we are confronted with a series of strong commands. The word "therefore" that begins verse 13 reminds us to look at the preceding context of 1:1–12 to learn more about how to live out those commands. Before God commands us to live holy lives, he does things that empower us to live that way.

¹³Therefore,

prepare your minds for action;

be self-controlled;

set your hope fully on the grace to be given

   you when Jesus Christ is revealed.

¹⁴As obedient children,

do not conform to the evil desires you

   had when you lived in ignorance.

¹⁵But just as he who called you is holy,

so be holy in all you do;

¹⁶for

it is written: "Be holy, because I am holy."

Read 1:1–12 carefully and note everything that God has already done for you that makes it possible for you to live a pure and holy life.

- We have been chosen by God (v. 2).
- We have been born to a living hope (v. 3).
-
-
-
-

   As you read what immediately comes after 1:13–16, you will notice that Scripture emphasizes again God's greatness (italicized) and goodness (underlined). We can't get away from God's holy love.

Other Kinds of Purity?
On the topic of purity, many people quickly think of the need for sexual purity, and rightly so. But we are called to "be holy in all [we] do." In what other areas of life is purity an urgent need?

¹⁷Since you call on <u>a Father</u> *who judges each man's work impartially, live your lives as strangers here in reverent fear.* ¹⁸For you know that it was <u>not with perishable things such as silver or gold that you were redeemed from the empty way of life handed down to you from your forefathers,</u> ¹⁹but with the precious blood of Christ, a lamb without blemish or defect.

The Temple

Or do you not know that your body is a temple of the Holy Spirit who is in you, whom you have from God, and that you are not your own? For you have been bought with a price: therefore glorify God in your body.

—1 Corinthians 6:19–20 NASB

Look again at 1 Peter 1:13–16 and observe any commands, comparisons, explanations, motivations, time references, and so on. Write what you see beside the passage on page 59.

What are your three most significant observations?

-
-
-

That tiny phrase "in all you do" stands tall. It refers not just to our behavior in religious settings, but to our whole way of life (Gal. 1:13; Eph. 4:22; Heb. 13:7; 1 Peter 1:18). Rather than holiness pulling us completely out of our society to hide in some "sacred" bubble, God commands us to be holy (closely connected to God) in all we do. We are to be holy in public and private, when we're working or playing, alone or in groups, on Sundays as well as Saturday nights. God calls us to be holy 24/7.

Crossing the Bridge

From your reading of the context and study of the passage, do you see any differences between Peter's original audience and us?

What are the timeless theological principles in 1 Peter 1:13–16 that connect with both the biblical audience and with us (the bridge between their town and ours)?

So What?

1. Do you think God's demand for holiness is unrealistic? Why or why not?

2. In what way has Becoming 3 helped you clarify your understanding of "holy"?

3. In what area of your life is "being holy" the most difficult struggle?

"prepare your minds for action"—This phrase literally reads "gird up the loins of your mind." In the ancient world when people needed to run fast or work hard, they had to gather up their long robes and tie them around their waist to avoid stumbling. "Mind" refers to our way of thinking or our understanding. The entire word picture reminds us that we are not playing games with God. Jesus calls us to be alert, poised for action, and focused on a single purpose.

"self-controlled"—This word means to be sober. Peter uses the same word in 4:7, where he urges us to stay sober so that we can pray, and in 5:8, where we are to be sober so that Satan won't defeat us. We automatically take this command as figurative (NASB even adds "in spirit" in 1:13; cf. 4:7; 5:8), but what Peter says in 4:1–3 and what Paul says in 1 Thessalonians 5:6–8 makes us think again.

"do not conform"—This word is found only one other place in the New Testament—Romans 12:2. The word carries the idea of being squeezed or forced into a mold. Before we came to Christ, we were shaped and molded by selfish desires for wealth, power, and pleasure. Peter warns us not to allow those former desires to control our lives now that we are Christians.

Cross-References

Lev. 11:44–45; 19:2; 20:7; Rom. 12:1–2; 1 Cor. 6:12–20; 1 Thess. 3:12–13; 4:3–8; 5:4–11; 1 Tim. 4:12; 2 Tim. 1:8–9; 2:20–21; Heb. 12:4–29; James 4:7–10; 1 Peter 2:9–12; 3:1–4; 4:1–3; 2 Peter 3:11–14; 1 John 1:5–10; 3:2–3

For Deeper Study

Arterburn, Stephen, and Fred Stoeker. *Every Man's Battle.* Colorado Springs: Water-Brook, 2000.

Bell, Rob. *Sex God: Exploring the Endless Connections Between Sexuality and Spirituality.* Grand Rapids: Zondervan, 2007.

Laaser, Mark. *Sexual Integrity in a Fallen World.* Grand Rapids: Zondervan, 1996.

Marshall, I. Howard. *1 Peter.* IVP New Testament Commentary. Downers Grove, IL: InterVarsity Press, 1991.

Winter, Lauren. *Real Sex: The Naked Truth About Chastity.* Grand Rapids: Brazos, 2005.

4. How do you usually react when you fail to act holy? How does God want you to respond to your own failure?

5. What practical steps can you take to guard yourself against falling into your "favorite" sin?

6. What more should the church do to help individual Christians live pure and holy lives?

Blomberg, Craig L. *1 Corinthians*. NIV Application Commentary. Grand Rapids: Zondervan, 1995.

Bonhoeffer, Dietrich. *Life Together*. San Francisco: HarperSanFrancisco, 1954.

Bruner, Frederick Dale. *The Christbook: Matthew 1–12*. Grand Rapids: Eerdmans, 1987.

Dorsett, Lyle W. *Seeking the Secret Place: The Spiritual Formation of C. S. Lewis*. Grand Rapids: Baker, 2004.

Duvall, J. Scott, and J. Daniel Hays. *Grasping God's Word: A Hands-On Approach to Reading, Interpreting, and Applying the Bible*. 2nd ed. Grand Rapids: Zondervan, 2005.

Erickson, Millard J. *Christian Theology*. 2nd ed. Grand Rapids: Baker, 1998.

Foster, Richard J. *Celebration of Discipline*. 25th anniversary ed. San Francisco: HarperSanFrancisco, 2003.

Giglio, Louie. *The Air I Breathe: Worship as a Way of Life*. Sisters, OR: Multnomah, 2003.

Hendricks, Howard G., and William D. Hendricks. *Living By the Book*. Revised and expanded. Chicago: Moody, 2007.

Hughes, Kent. *Acts: The Church Afire*. Wheaton: Crossway, 1996.

Larson, Craig Brian, ed. *Choice Contemporary Stories and Illustrations for Preachers, Teachers, and Writers*. Grand Rapids: Baker, 1998.

———. *Illustrations for Preaching and Teaching*. Grand Rapids: Baker, 1993.

Lewis, C. S. *The Four Loves*. Glasgow: William Collins, 1960.

———. *Mere Christianity*. New York: Macmillan, 1952.

Long, Jimmy. *Emerging Hope: Strategy for Reaching Postmodern Generations*. 2nd ed. Downers Grove, IL: InterVarsity Press, 2004.

Lucado, Max. *The Great House of God*. Dallas: Word, 1997.

McGrath, Alister E. *Understanding the Trinity*. Grand Rapids: Zondervan, 1988.

Miller, Don. *Blue Like Jazz: Nonreligious Thoughts on Christian Spirituality*. Thorndike, ME: Thorndike, 2006.

Ortberg, John. *Everybody's Normal Till You Get to Know Them*. Grand Rapids: Zondervan, 2003.

Press, Bill. *Spin This: All the Ways We Don't Tell the Truth*. New York: Simon and Schuster, 2002.

Roberts, Mark D. *Dare to Be True: Living in the Freedom of Complete Honesty*. Colorado Springs: Waterbrook, 2003.

Stott, John R. W. *Authentic Christianity: From the Writings of John Stott*. Ed. Timothy Dudley-Smith. Downers Grove, IL: InterVarsity Press, 1996.

Willard, Dallas. *Renovation of the Heart*. Colorado Springs: NavPress, 2002.

J Scott Duvall is professor of New Testament at Ouachita Baptist University, a Christian liberal-arts college in Arkansas, where he teaches Spiritual Formation, Interpreting the Bible, Greek, and New Testament Studies. He received his B.A. from Ouachita and his M.Div. and Ph.D. from Southwestern Seminary, and has been teaching at OBU since 1989. He also serves as copastor of Fellowship Church of Arkadelphia, Arkansas.

Duvall's other publications include *Grasping God's Word*, *Journey into God's Word*, *Preaching God's Word*, *Biblical Greek Exegesis*, *The Story of Israel*, *The Dictionary of Biblical Prophecy and End Times*, and *Experiencing God's Story of Life and Hope: A Workbook for Spiritual Formation*.